Boundless Voices

-Poetry Rex-

By **ERIC KYALO**

Moncheri Romance

Asia. Africa. Europe

Title of Book: **Boundless Voices**
Author of Book: **Eric Kyalo**
First Published in India in April 2022 by Moncheri Romance

ISBN 13: 978-93-93695-63-5

Published & Printed by
Moncheri Romance
Noel Lorenz House of Fiction
Headquarters - Kolkata, West Bengal, India
154A, KCG Road, Kolkata - 700050
www.noellorenz.com

About Book

Boundless voices are an invaluable aid designed to harness posy into one broad and easy to follow text. This all-encompassing approach aims at affording readers of poesy a clearer grasp of this genre. Efforts of all these poets will go a long way in providing the reader with a better understanding of all aspects of poesy which proves that poesy is world's secret weapon in the way that the oral culture is interwoven into written poems, to be enjoyed for education as well as a good read. It is through poesy where readers meet and relate with vast occurrences from around the African communities.

INTRODUCTION

A vigorous and informed selection has ensured that it combines the confidence of classics with the freshness that contemporary poets bring their craft. This anthology has featured all great poets in all parts of Kenya and to some extend outside Kenya. Some of the poets featured here are from EADtv, Surpass, Destiny International recognized universities and other areas of education.

Destiny Ink Splinter Production makes this anthology a store which stores poems which seek to entertain, provoke, empower and educate. Themes portrayed in different poems are as wide ranging as poet's backgrounds but they share a common belief – enhancing values of integrity in today's society in effort to preserve human and social dignity. It is through this anthology that Destiny Ink Splinter Production makes us understand fruits which come with tribal and racial tolerance. This is why this anthology was compiled by Eric – to show how different tribes can be united and be made one. This is one of anthologies that have overcame tribal boundaries. Poems contained in this anthology were written by different poets from different birth places, places of work, places of study and places of adventures. They have then collaborated to bring out similarities and differences from those places.

Boundless voices are an invaluable aid designed to harness posy into one broad and easy to follow text. This all-encompassing approach aims at affording readers of poesy a clearer grasp of this genre. Efforts of all these poets will go a long way in providing the reader with a better understanding of all aspects of poesy which proves that poesy is world's secret weapon in the way that the oral culture is interwoven into written poems, to be enjoyed for education as well as a good read. It is through poesy where readers meet and relate with vast occurrences from around the African communities.

(Doris Mukami)

ERIC KYALO

Born in Machakos county, Kenya, where he underwent many early struggles for emancipation, Successively a poet, a writer, a public speaker, a counselor and a mentor. He is one of the teen writers bringing fame to Kenyan literature. He travels widely and has been acclaimed as a writer, an academic and an inspiration. His interests are in literature and motivation.

Author of great talent; - his works include – Chronicles of a Poet, Blazes of Love, Torch of success, In your hands lie your destiny. Revival and Navigating Youthful Encounters.

1.DESPAIR NOT

Son, you'll live to battle another day

Don't despair in thy battle

I can sense thy exhaustion and growing exasperation

That gives thee nonchalant carelessness

And wreck ling of thy naïve heart

This makes thee befuddle thyself

With weird kind of reasoning

Son, you'll live to battle another day

Dazed fleeting impression has registered

On thy awareness

Due to havoc in thy already

Troubled life

Caused by despondency and downheartedness

Altering in thy naive heart

Failure is standing at the door way

Grinning down at you surely

Boundless Voices

Only blood and marrow grants thee

Sustenance to live

You'll live to battle another day

2.WEEP NOT

Son, days are passing when people

Demeaned you

Take heart and focus on thy tiny dreams

Delude this monster that is failure

Once more, keep thy screams restrained.

Weep not my dear son

Don't let me bear thy sobs

Don't even let me bear the growling

The rumbling kvetch of thy agony

Wrestle a brute like failure

And gather fragmented pieces of thy

Dream

Where you' ll muster thy courage

To alleviate from thy overwhelmed

ecstatic feelings

Boundless Voices

Don't lose focus in this gallant battle

Despite it having a glow of dark

Crimson

That reaches thy horizon to detriment

Once again, weep not my dear son.

3. BEATRACE, MY GRANDMOTHER

Beatrice, my grandmother

You know very well I'm a ringer

For I am worthy this journey

I can confidently view my life like a masque

This makes me a literature jock

Beatrice, my grandmother

You made me a four- square monhre

In my exquisite jaunt as a jawan

Who has finished the races?

I still have to keep souring

Beatrice, my grandmother

It infuriated me, when mama deserted me,

With her inimical policy to my interests

Which made me nuzzle up against thee

Just to get solace

Beatrice, my grandmother

When momma deserted me

With her thought that I'm a clumsy oaf

Who is feeble minded

You was my source of hope and confidence

Who neither detested nor disillusioned me

Beatrice, my grandmother

You have always inspired me

That God cannot allow this suffering

Be meted upon my life's journey

Even if my fouls use dodgy methods

God will hear my cry

And one day I shall drink a cup of espresso

As a kind of gesture of what God

Shall have done in my life

4.WHY KAMBA?

Why Kambas?

Why do thee bewitch themselves?

Why at very sight of thy sons do you

 Enrage them?

To make their living remain unwelcomed

And detested

To make them grow up sullen, bewildered and resentful.

Why do you bewitch they mongrels and lasses?

Thyself doubt makes them awkward

And very difficult to deal with

In everything they do.

This is why Kambas you never share national cake.

You'll forever live to be ruled by

 Other tribes

Boundless Voices

Why do we have businesses allover?

The country except in Kambaland

Is it that we don't have rich tycoons?

Are we not children of generation of?

Masaku and chief Kisoi

It is only that we bewitch ourselves.

Are we not children of generation of?

Kisoi Munyao

Who defeated all Kenyan tribes?

And Europeans

To climb Mount Kenya to plant flag

Of independence

Are not born champions and winners?

It is only that we bewitch each other.

Kambas hamper this archaic practice

Be mongrels and lasses full of love

Boundless Voices

Wish your branches all the best

And empower them

Ukambani should be given a deference and honor

Curtail bewitching yourselves

So as to see a great nation in yourselves

5.JAMHURI DAY

A day full of peace and calm

A day of beauty and charm

A day of leadership; a day of sovereignty

A day of love and a day of joy

A day new Kenya was born

A day Eric was born

 A day the great poet and author

Got into land full of agonies

A day Eric cries, a day Kenya rejoices

A day Eric stretches, a day Kenya dances

A day Kenya signs in the land and in air

Praises of a new start everywhere

A great day we all celebrate

Adulating the great power in the world

Boundless Voices

Brave heroes maintained, souls filled with joy

Bravery and courage, tongues profess.

Jamhuri day is a lovely book

A book full of greatness

A day of self independence

A day of new beginning

Brave heroes maintained, souls filled with joy

Boundless Voices

John Wesley Atetwe

He is a Kenyan born poet, who loves poetry because it is a God given talent. He was born and raised in Kenya with a goal to change this world making a better place not only for him but also for the next generation. He believes that through his gift, God will help him achieve this goal as Philippians 4:13 states that " I can do all things through Christ   who strengthens me…"

1.Watchers' prayer day 6

Adoration

Father Lord today I come before you
Dedicating the heavens unto you
Because everything in heaven and on earth
They all belong to you
Ebenezer I bless the heavens
I bless you my Maker
O Lord you're amazing
Your work is magnificent

Elohim you deserve to be glorified
You deserve to be adored
You're God today and forever
O my Lord your kingdom reigns forever
You're awesome my God
You're so amazing
You're powerful
You always manifest your power lord
Your kingdom come
Thy will be done on earth
You're omniscient
You're omnipresent
You're sweet my lord
I worship you Jehovah
I sing hallelujah my lord
You're the prince of peace

Because by you kings reign
Rulers issue decrees that are just.

Through your power
I've seen the sick being healed
I've seen the lame walk
Indeed you're the soon coming king
Through you I've seen saints
Through you I've seen miracles
Through you I've seen prophets
Through you I've seen
The manifestation of tongues
Through you I've seen intercessors
O my God you're amazing
Glory and honor belongs to you Abba

Receive the praises Lord
Receive the glory Lord
Receive the adoration my Maker
I love you my God
You're super amazing
You're so wonderful
I give you glory my God
In the name of Jesus Christ
Thank you Jesus, thank you redeemer in Jesus name

Amen

2. Diana – The pageant Queen
You were born with gift
I'm proud for it in you
All I can say you're gifted
For you always tell me
Patience and hard work pays
Indeed it's true Diana
I'm proud of you my noble poetess
Congratulations to you miss county

The pageant Queen of Kitui County
This is a blessing not only to you
But also to your parents
Diana Masaa
Congratulations
Remember the sky is the limit
There's no limit to ambitions
Diana this is just the beginning
You're now started
Remember to put God first

I remember you walked on the stage
With a majestic courage
And I saw God on your side
His favor was on you Diana
You made us proud
Till the adjudicators were all amazed
Miss County you're amazing
You're the pride of Kitui

Boundless Voices

All I can say is you're going far
May this gift take you places?
May it open doors for you
As it is in the scriptures
A man's gift makes room for him
And brings him before great men
May it be so in Jesus Name?
May you go internationally?
Through this pageantry

May you find favor before God?
May you find favor before men?
May you reign and be the
Queen of Africa

I'm so proud of you
You're the pride of Kenya
I see greatness in you dear
You will do it dear
And you'll be the jiving testimony
May God be on your side?
Congratulations Diana
The pageant queen

3.Watcher's prayer day 7

Encounter
Lord Jesus today I'm here
I'm presenting my heart
As a sacrifice
I'm offering myself to you
As a deity
For you're my joys over my life
Lord Jesus you're my savior
Lord Jesus you're my portion
Lord Jesus you're my every thing
I love you Jesus, I love you Jesus.

I want to say thank you
Thank you for being with me
Thank you for the gift of life
Thank you for the abundant blessings
Thank you for this gift Ebenezer
You're amazing my Lord
You're wonderful
Adinai I exalt you my father
I exalt you my maker

Let this day be of an encounter
I want an encounter with you
May it be so Jesus?
I ask for a double portion
Like that of Elisha

Boundless Voices

Be with me to the end Lord
Let it low in all portions

Lord I need a flow of mantles
A diversity of mantles
Whether it's a worship mantle
Whether it's a poetic mantle
Whether it's a singing mantle
Let it flow in all dimensions
For this is an encounter
A diversity of mantles Jesus
May your will be done

Let this be unforgettable experience
Because I believe in miracles
I believe in you
Just as you said in Jeremiah 33:3
Call unto me and I will answer thee
And show the great things
And mighty things which
Though knowest not
Lord may your will be done
Thank you for this encounter
I worship you lord in Jesus name
I pray and believe

Amen

4. The pageantry Queen

Congratulation Diana
You made it again
Your family is so proud of you
I'm also proud of you
I see God's grace upon you
You're a super model
For this is your God given gift
Keep it up, keep it up

O Diana the pride of Kitui County
The lade from Ukambani
Endowed with the beauty of God
You're a super model
I'm very proud of you
Keep it up
You were born to win
For the Lord's favor is upon you
You were born to conquer

From Machakos to Vihiga county
I can see you've got the potential
Let me call you miss county
For you've made me proud
And I believe one day
You'll be the pride of Kenya
This is just the beginning
The game has now begun
The red carpet was you arena

Boundless Voices

Everyone was astonished
With your beautiful moves
You're super amazing
You're a celebrity
You're my icon
Diana Masaa the pride of Kitui
Congratulations keep it up

May you move from county to county?
May you go internationally?
May your gift bring you before men?
May God locate you?
I decree favor in your life
In the name of Jesus Christ
May you find favor everywhere you go?
I see greatness in you Diana
Keep it up, keep it up
I'm so proud of you.

5. Beauty of Ashes, Isaiah 61;3

It's going to be an encounter
It's going to be a blessing
For this is what the lord says
This is a message for his children
God is going to restore them
God is going to lift you
It does not matter what
You've been through
It does not matter what
You're going through

This is going to be your year
This is going to be your mantle
This is going to be your testimony
The testimony of beauty of ashes
For the lord is with you
This is a declaration
Remember his word never comes back void
But it must fulfill what God desires

For the lord will provide
For those who grieve in Zion
The lord will bestow on them
 A crown of beauty instead of ashes
The lord will bestow on them
The oil of joy instead of mourning
The lord will bestow on them

Boundless Voices

A garment of praise instead of spirits of despair
They will be called oaks of righteousness
 A planting of the lord
For the display of his splendor
That's what the lord says

It's going to be an encounter
Your life will never be the same
This is you years
That's what the lord says
He will raise you again trust in Him
He will lift you up
You'll dance with joy for his miracles
God is going to surprise you
You'll be singing " I made it through"
That will be your anthem
For this encounter
My God is amazing, he never disappoints.

DICKSON IMBUYE

He is a Kenyan co- Author a poet and a lover of literature. He is currently a student in Jomo Kenyatta University pursuing Electrical and Electronic Engineering. Besides literature; technology is one of his
biggest interests.

1.SWIFT JOURNEY

My soul is awakened, and
Its own happiness deprived
My spirit is souring, like a
Wandering caravan
And carried aloft on the
Wings of the breeze
Above me, around me
 Everything seems to be roaring
And my heart's peace tormenting

The long withered grass
In the sunshine is glancing
While the bare long trees
Are tossing high their branches
My breathe turns a mile
Into a non- manageable pain
The dead leaves beneath
 The ground are dancing
Mocking my feary eyes
And broken my rage
I wish I could see how the
 Ocean is lashing
Well my eyes can see
Everything except for the
Understanding

Before I wave goodbyes
To the living nature,
I will kneel in awe-stuck
Silence
Gently trembling as I wait
In the glory and grace
Found in everything he
 Created
Unassisted
Unencumbered
As my mysteries unfold back
So will my judgment follow me

2.SUPER WOMAN

God blessed us with you super mum
You are perfect in form
I wish I could take you to Rome
For you deserve nothing
But the best especially
 From me your son

You whispered words of hope
At my low moments
I wish you many happy returns
On the face of earth's lens
I take to my pen
Because words are the only way
I can

God bless you mama bear
You gave us a chance to life bare
Indoctrinated us will well
Needed values in our lair
Now we are upstanding
Denizens because of your care

It's only fair that I return the favor as I say, I love you
You and only you
I am glad Dad said I do
To such a lovely woman
That he woed

Boundless Voices

Without you we are nothing
With you were something
Like a dose of bathing
I will always need you in my life
Even when I'm not lurking

Lovely mama
Bubby mummy
Daring mommy
May mungu give you a long life?
Mamaa
That you may see the
Man you gave birth to
And the returns I always
Crave to give you.

3.Whispers in the dark

A mind wandering
 Through catacombs of insanity
Am so deprived of humanity
Lunging and waiting for one
Merciful death eagerly
Hoping it arrives early
A victim of catastrophe,
 Torn up by strife

Am slowly driven away
By feelings of hungry madness
Overgrown by consuming coldness
Listen to my heartbeats,
Slowly painting down in – rubbed
Limericks
Demanding the last tone of
 Breath so anxious
With dim hope it comes with
 No pains
My senses are roaming in blinding
Emptiness
Scenes filled with horrifying absurdness
This is a deserted life bonded to unwanted loneliness
A place populated with demonic
Owls

My heart now beats steady in
Rhythms of hatred
Blurred thought, sick and so much
 Twisted
Painful destructive sorrow that never
 Ended
The ongoing delirium in darkness
 Is my prison cell
Whispers of music from a far
But the lyrics of all songs
 Are not mine

4.Tonight

I have a plan, to ran away tonight
I will escape my own fights and find
Peace within
I will curl up and forget all the haunting
 Of my dark soul
Tonight I will give myself another
 New identity
Not a doll
Not a massacre of loud demons
But a jewel to be adored and well owned.

Yes, tonight I will stay calm and find
A soundtrack for my demons to dance
The peaceful tune
I will shun away from those fights
That leave me in a broken mess
I will jump in a candle- lighted abyss
 For the rest of the night

I will close my eyes to every scene
That render me fearful
I will block my thoughts from the
Painful reality
Tonight, I want to stay so obvious
If it will take me screaming for hours
Jokes all along or laughing the whole night
As long as my haunting stay away

Tonight I will avoid shattering in a corner
I will not battle with myself
I won't try to solve my mystery
I will let all the dotted life stream
 Remain scary
I will please only myself with deep
Breath

If the morning finds me well
I will hold on to memories of this
 One peaceful night and be stronger
 Enough to fight again.
For that's what fate decided for me.

5.DRUG

I didn't fall for her first
Nope, I learnt to trust her
With all my instincts
I learnt to share all of me with her first
Even though I have had trust issues all my life
I felt safe with her
I didn't have walls around her
She was a friend, she was a family
She was a simple innocent relation first

I recall our first meeting
She was silent, never loud and intrusive
There was a hidden alienation around her
Yet like a moth to flame I was silently
 Drawn
I was intrigued to touch and see if the fire

Burned and so I walked a little closer

I felt warm and addictive
 Like sweet flowing honey
It was pure and sweet

So I got tempted to walk a little closer
I wasn't searching to own
It was never about taking all of her
Nay, it was always about the little precious moments she
spent around

Boundless Voices

It was always about the times she was silent yet warm and
scorching

Her scent wasn't the loud, kind
Nope, it was the silent seemingly elusive
Kind
It was the kind that slowly makes itself
 Into your skin
The kind that had no dirt on it
It began from simple talks
The kind that marked the rise of dawn

And just like a wave
She intruded me more
She learned how to handle me better
Our indulgence and obsession was more
 Than addiction.

A drug

6.Shards

I   worked non tirelessly to become her one
Kind of man
I learned to mask the man in me
I finally became the he she loved most
I learned and later approved to let go of
 What I loved
I only loved what she loved
I loved what she loved
I loved her, I did all it takes to be
 Her perfect man

Every morning I learnt to put on a smile
Even though she got it wrong
I learnt how to unmask her smile and
Did it to y level best
I laughed with my bleeding heart and
Played of jokes at my expense of mystery

I will never blame her
No she was never the problem
It is me I look back and shame
Overshadow me
I wander why I did love her so much
And forgot to love myself

I envy myself again
For I was that strong to let myself leave and be another for
her
I forgot my identity so quick and took hers
I don't always understand
So I smile and laugh at myself pity I hold

I still remember so nights I sat still
For hours I sat by the doors waiting
I held my phone, fully charged
As always waited for her call
Even a single text could ignite the warm
 Short hair
I remember smiling and laughing for the
 Messages she sent me
I remember feeling that loving her was so
 Right
Maybe she knew I was breaking
We were two halves a whole but my part
Seemed not to matter
Maybe that's why she knew me better

I remember when I finally shed tears
Big men don't cry
I felt disappointed and broken
It wasn't because I knew I was sinking
I cried so hard when she said "sorry"
Sorry for the pain she never meant to cause
Sorry for the times I felt not so right

Boundless Voices

Sorry for the mornings the sun felt so alien
Sorry for the times light was another mystery

That night I did cry
I felt so unworthy
I did feel like loving her wasn't wrong
And that's why she was my rise and downfall
That's why she is my kind of drug
Sweet and so addictive

LOVEEN KALYA

She is a Kenyan born student and citizen. She takes bachelor of Education (Civil Engineering) at Masinde Muliro University in her second year. She's a poetess, actores and talented in drawing

1.Jail break

A light is said to be at the end o the tunnel
But it is also outside the tunnel
Break that tunnel
Remove those cuffs
Break the chains
Unlock that lock
Get out, look outside
There's a lot of light there
The sun has risen
New hope has come
The dark is gone
And so are all the bad things
Get out of that box
Explore be open minded
Learn new things
Place those fears down for a second
And let you be a free ion
Don't be mind- fixed
Be mind free

2.Listen

The sound of silence
Hear oh hear this sound of silence
This loud voice coming out of it
Listen to this please
Hear their pleas I plead

Listen
To the voices of the orphans
Hear what they can't put to words
"we are human too you know"
" we deserve love and affection"
Hear oh hear, I need your ear
To these street livers and refugees
Widows, widowers, amputees
Those struggling to make ends meet
Those trying to reach their hands
To their mouths

Hear oh hear how I plea
The voices of those victims you
 Don't want to see
Of fire, drought, famine, war,
 Floods, conflicts, rape,
Name them all
Listen to their hearts crying
Listen to the voices they can't speak
Listen to their loud silence

Boundless Voices

Hear oh hear I cry to you please
The voice of graduates unemployed
Waiting for those 'jobs' they were
 Promised
Stop watching in silence
Listen oh listen, this is my plea
To this loud sound of silence

3.My daughter

Am a mess
19 but 've been through
There's a lot I wanna tell you
But know that momma loves you
Am still young and not
 Ready for you now
Don't know if you'll come but
When you do
I want you to know this
You're beautiful, let no one tell
You that or otherwise
You're strong, independent
You're perfect just as you are
You're enough
Let no one take your innocence
Let no one speed your maturity
Let no one take advantage of you
Of your kindness of purity
I'd love you to be aggressive,
Creative, curious
Tough, fearless, confident, brave
Every good thing
Not like me
Don't be afraid to go for
 What you want
Men are just men
And so are women

Boundless Voices

I want you to be you
Don't be afraid to be weird
Don't be afraid to do your thing
And most of all
Don't let down your guard
I don't want you to regret
a thing
Not like me
Be kind but not weak
Be gentle but not stupid
Let your toughness come from within
And, baby girl
For as long as am alive
I got you

4.My son

Dear son
I've walked on thorns and hot coal
Not literally, you're bright enough
To understand
I've seen muscles and touched packs
Felt how biceps feel
Witnessed different kinds of strengths
I've seen veins and arteries
Heard voices from the deepest base
But son being a man is more
 Than all these
Live your own life, a happy one
Be humble and tough
And always on your knees
To the greatest father
It'd be great for you my baby boy
To be a gentleman
Be willing to go out of your way
 For others
Be kind, courteous and Wise
I don't imply that you don't get
 Muscles and a deep voice
No
I want you to have muscles
Right from within
But don't let these skirts
And tight trousers to take advantage of you

Boundless Voices

Spend but be wise
Save and invest
And when you find a good woman
Take good care of her
They are rare
Momma loves you

5.Shadowy hero

The battle is over but not the war
I will not put down my sword
Neither will I sit but stand
I will stand firm to defend
Watch, patrol not pretend
For I know not the origin
Of these wars
Neither do I know
Its whereabouts and direction
Just as no one knows that of the sun
So until am sure you're safe I will stand
Give you my hand
As you celebrate and throw you lamps
I vow peace to you will revamps
For I will fight
Do it with all my might
Never let you out of my sight
This to you is my plight
I will be your light

LEON JOSEPH OMONDI

He is a Kenyan poet and lover of literature. He was born in Siaya County and raised up in south Gem. He was taught poetry by Emmanuel Cheret (Prince Diaries). One of the famous Kenyan poets. He has made love poetry his products.

1.Soon it will be over.

The pain of losing your love
The love of your life
One like no other
More than your better half
The one that mean the world
To you
It really hits different

She was my joy
She kept me lovely
She made me smile
And laugh every time she
Cracked her jokes
A best teacher she was
A role model and caring
Mother
I really feel empty without her next to me

Who is gonna replace her
No, I don't think there's any
A mother like her I can't find
Her love was much more
Ker kindness, giving me
The first priority in every
Positive way,
Mommy hope you get my cry
My tears rolls down my cheek

Boundless Voices

Daily
I really miss you mommy

With hopes that we shall meet
 Again
I carry on like a man
Hoping to die soon, so
 That I may see you again
I guess you resting in peace
And soon I'll get over this
 And it will be over
Rest in peace mommy

2.Am sorry

I am very sorry,
Very sorry I wasn't there for you
Very sorry I never showed up
Showed up after…….
We had messed up

Am sorry I left
And all the burden you carried
Verily I was fake
And all the shame you bore on my
 Behalf
Very sorry for a little mother I made you

But again am happy
Am happy you never got rid of her
And for nine months you carried her
And a charming princes she is
With beauty just like you

Again am very sorry
And on your knees I kneel
For my guilt keep pinching me,
And your forgiveness I seek
I really pity myself for my deeds
and being irresponsible
I beg get a place in your heart and forgive me

Boundless Voices

Still my baby mamah
Mamah
And another chance I seek
Responsible father I swear I'll be
Offer me this chance at least to see
 Her smile
For that I've been lunging for
Please let her know am her Daddy
 While you her Mummy
Please I beg

I know I messed up
But just understand life was hard then
Let's reunite and make a happy family
For that's what a beautiful woman
 Like you deserves
And my Queen you will always be

3.TILL DEATH DO US APART

Till death do us apart
Yes I promise you my love
Yes I promise you happiness
Yes I promise you protection and care
Yes I do and on your figure I place a ring

I chose you from a million
And I'll always make you the one
Your beauty kills me
And I'll never let you go
You will always be my best woman
 Me as your best man

Kissing in front of everyone
Walking like love birds in town
When they all us Mr and Mrs Omondi
That's the feeling am craving for
Being the best couple in the town
Yeah that one

So it's till death do us apart
I'll always love you
I'll always cherish you
I'll always make you
My first priority and my favorite woman
For a wonderful queen you are
My lost rib
All my love I give unto you

Boundless Voices

4.My love

Your touch
Your smile
That tooth gap
Your fine chest
Leave alone your fine curves
Jabber, you really……
You really win my heart
And my love am ready to give

Your melodious voice
When you call me
Your sexy eyes when you look at me
Your soft touch when you meet my skin
Leave alone your sugary lips
When you kiss me Rambayana
You really drive me crazy
And this kind of love so sweet
On my throne you sit
A queen to me you are

The taste of your delicious meal
The neatness of your room
How you iron your clothes
How you match your dressing code
Leave alone how you spread your bed
Not forgetting how you wake me up
Nyamwalo, a wife material you are

Boundless Voices

My number one I rank you
For mama watoto I got
And good mother you are
I can see
Our love is so strong
Letting you go, they won't see

5.My Pride

Jabber Nyamwalo
Life with you is my pride
You being by my side
You really mean the world to me
Having you with our kids
Is just a blessing

I am always happy with you
We play like kids
When lynn and leaky
Plays with toys
We crack jokes
As they smile
And we laugh together as a
 family

Nyamamana
You are my best
You brought heaven to earth for me
You solved all my problems
And made me your king
As I ranked you my queen
The pride of the lake of the region
Life with you is more than a fantasy.

6.If the world allows

If the world still allows me
If he still let me live
If we can still get to see new days
And get to grow day to day
I swear I won't change my love

I will still show the world
How much I love you
I will let them know how I
 Really adore you
And their girlfriends are nothing
 Before you

If my mum asks for a daughter – in- law
I won't hesitate to introduce you
 for my ribs you are
Don't forget you marry I Joseph
A perfect match we are

The future of my kids I choose
And a good mother to them you are
For the Mother Nature I detected in you
Humbled and always smart
My mama watoto I got

MERCY KALYA

She is a Kenyan poet, writer ,vocalist and thespian — currently pusuing Acturial science at Mount Kena University. She believes there is more to everything and everyone than just the surface view; look beyond the cover

1.Hello

Hello
Welcome to another instalment of my life
I know you never asked for an update
But like an online creator
I'll give it anyway
I'm still alone
Walk alone, sit alone, sleep alone
Only a few hours older than yesterday
But feeling so much older
I still crave validation
My patience needs medication
Afraid to try some meditation
Trauma is my life's hydration
Too much of something is poisonous?
I refuse to give into that adage
Maybe I will when like those who said it
I'm deep into my old age
I still live in constant denial
My job still sucks as it used to
I now measure success
As the number of days I get through

2. Take it

Her job was to shut up and take it
Whether her will or not the least bit
Ignore the cruel days by the sight
of the ring
And tied down, severed her on good wing
Forced to take all jobs and punches
Forced to rid all her intuitive hunches
Sots at the table but will never rank higher
For what she cannot change always under
 Fire
Ever dreading the approach of faceless perverts
Ever bearing the pressure society to a woman
 Exerts
Her job is to keep mum and take it
Force a smile just because he likes it
Her job is to feign hope, somehow cope
Just grope
Not one stop

3.Broken

Sweet as honey
Dear amnesia
I send you this letter of request
So that you come into my head
And erase all memory of my negative
Let only love and care be left there
All humanity, high magnitude humility
And maybe a little pinch of pride
To keep my soul moistly watered
Take away remembrance from my being
Take away my name as well
But keep the light of love alive
Let me feel what is meant by pure
To see not my flaws but my capabilities
Your aspiring friend
A broken soul

4. One more fight

'At ease'
Is what they said
'Fighting battles is what you do
'Attention'
The voice was raised
'From here life is to hear and do'
That was all before
Now
Now I stand alone
Motivation gone
Wars in my head
Disturbed by what's said
Body steady
Weapons ready
But the fight is not physical
The commands are not oral
I'm constantly on the edge
O top of the world but about to fall off the edge
Ever in an unstable stage
About to my life trade as a wage
To the gods they believe in
Without a thought to win
As many hands do nothing
Mind too simple yet complex being
Just one more
One more sound of their riffles' cocking
One more command to charge on heels

One more rush of her death living
Maybe then it takes my
lost soul heal......

5. Not really
No… I'm not okay
Thanks for asking
But I'm sure my bad days
Are nothing to you
I'm not okay
But my problems are not your cup of steap
My mind keeps switching off
Living on autopilot for the past year
That's not something you care about
No ……not really
I'm not really fine
Though that's my answer every time
And every time it leaves me questioning
Am I really fine
So no…..I'm not okay

JAMES NZIVO MUTHINI

He was born in 13/01/1999 in Makima ward, Mbeere south constituency, Embu county. He is an undergraduate at Kenya Methodist University (Meru) doing English and literature. Besides writing poems , he writes criticles and critiques.

He has written " Kenya at coming to birth and the 21st Generation in Love"

1. Death! Death!
Death! Death! Death! It has come
No pity, no reason, no request
It automatically comes
It has come, death we fear you much
Accept it, for we are all candidates

A mother, a father, a child
A delinquent, a noble
Death fears no any, it's brave enough
How courageous are you death?
Accept it, for we are all candidates

Unlearned, bachelors, PhDs and profs
Death takes away every level, alrighty?
Mourning and weeping
It leaves people grieving
Accept it, for we are all candidates

2.Die hard
I'm an orphan my parents passed
Am a hustler
I survive by God's grace
I'll never give up

I'm a widow
my husband is underground
I can't withstand when they talk or sneeze
I'll never give up

I'm a slave
After my parents passed
Sisters, brothers and the youngest are slaves too
I'll never give up

Am a landless, and a peasant
A farm I inherited
Ferocious creatures took it
I hustle to buy a point
I'll never give up
I have two cattle
Ferocious I'm still salivating
Where will I go?
I'll die hard

I'll never give up

3. My son

Hear me! My son
I'm you mother, I bore you
Look at me, learn something
Oloo! Hear me

Life is very strange, I tell you
We are still climbing endurin'
Facing many challenges, daily
Oloo! Hear me

Go to school and learn, Oloo
I wasted my opportunities, change not to be like me
The school I went, sneaking with other girls
Oloo! Hear me

You will see 'gold' will entice you
My son, I was once like them
Alas! I wish I knew
Oloo! Hear me

Alas! This was but a regretful thinking
I wish I could be aware, I could work hard
Life is toothless, but bites excruciatingly
Oloo! Hear me

Education is the key; your life is locked!
Your life will divert, stay vigilant!
Emancipate yourself, life isn't easy
Oloo! Be wise

4. My country

My country, I love you
My country I'll fight for you
My country I'll never forsake you
All days of my life, I swear

We brag of your economy, superb
Our agricultural products, high quality
Splendid and magnificent, they work
My country you're healthy and wealth

Poachers, hunters and bad gathers
Are deteriorating your productivity and
 Biodiversity
Flourished environment
Beautiful as they look
My country, you look awesome
They try to diminish your prestige
Through combative vices they do
Through reasonable facts they defy
My country you will perish
Roads, elegant sceneries and recreational areas
They all glitter! My country wow!
Everyday some beauty fades
My country you perish

The entire environment is ever green
Aesthetic is admirable by all citizens
Seasons change, citizens also change
Nature is destroyed,
My country I pity you

5.The new compound

The day has come, for me to leave
My father calls me, to prepare quickly
I smile while bathing
A new compound, I visited truly
I couldn't believe it

My mum calls,' Henry prepare adequately
I smile while dressing
My fellows had already reported
My siblings were not around truly
I was overwhelmed

The hired drive calls, "Henry do quickly"
I smile looking for my new socks
My cousin too is anxious to carry
 my box
Truly, it was the day

The journey starts, my heartbeat doubles
On the way he says, "Henry you have to work hard"
My mum iterates
"Henry you've to over work"
Truly, experience of a new compound
was nice

Boundless Voices

The principal came in the evening
Shivering and fear paralyzes me,
Heartbeat escalates, blood flow sounds
Hardening myself not to collapse
It was a confounding experience
Truly, I experienced a new experience
in the compound

OYUGI PHILIP

Philip is a young poet from Homabay, Kenya. He stared writing in 2018 where he released four collections of poetry on wattpad and one anthology on Amazon.

He is currently a student at Kisii University

1. Butterfly doors

She said
She found her soul
Mix of religion, little drops of spirituality
 me, I'm just watching from an atheist eye
She found God, But her actions makes me doubt;
It's existence entirely
The third entity of her soul
So plugged into the universe
I'm drinking little I can get from her soul
She found herself she writes
Her eyes cry blue
Her words paint happy
But there's a little darkness in her thoughts
She struggles with her personality a bit
But I try to hold on to her

She said
She found the divine feminine
The third eye to her physical form
I just want to touch the sweetness she drips
She leaves me in gaps
She meditates with the morning dew
She sings the space melodies
Makes me smile with my midnight pain
My horror dreams, with her visions
She's painting the world
She moves like a god

Boundless Voices

Conversations deep
I get drunk, in tune with her vibration
She whispers in my ear softly
"Hold my hands, we are going on ad adventure
Day turn to night
Turn off the light,
Drink deep from my soul
Kiss my lips with a soft touch

She said
She hears the universe talk
The alien whispers
She has got gifts from other world,
Beauty from the other side
Picture of her face
Lonely she appears
She got this ribe
This aesthetic, of a force that hooks my
Soul
She holds all of me,
The alley walk, with the street lights
When we hold hands,
I get high in her presence,
Her aroma like the morning music,
Slow beats with therapy
I'm lost in her presence
Let me not sink deep

Boundless Voices

2.It begins
You seek validation instead of truth
Religion instead of spirituality
Ego instead of yourself
You take instead of giving
Simple knowledge

As I hold this pen and paper
Reflecting on my life
The horrors I go through the night
The pain I see when the sky falls
Smiling when the sun is up
It gets dimmer with each down

Waking up with a frown and a yawn
I check myself
It's another day, time to hate my self
Put on that mask
Walk through the crowds and dust
Tell everything is alright
But I'm locked in a cage

Inside my brain
I see walls, with water
Am drowning, somebody hold my hand
Before I'm gone
Maybe I will, before that time
Let me write my story in a minute

Boundless Voices

See I've been holding myself
Seeing from the outside in
Fighting my soul to breathe
The demons make me feel weak
Am lost
The deep end
With fist fights

I feel tired sometimes
Sleep escapes my mind
In the darkest hours of time
The picture is dark
So is my face
These words that I breathe
Sitting down, under this tree
The journey begins

3.Hey Lucy

People like me – have the darkest minds
Poets like me- have the darkest rhymes
I try to smile, laugh,
Whenever I see your smile

Good grief – glorious dead
Mysterious smile, under the grass
The colours swirl, she asks who I am
The darkest days, sometimes I want out

She told me, hold on child, I see the light
 behind
Your eyes, the dreams shine don't die
Hold on to my grip feels the rapture
Let your soul crumble
When I touch your mind

You and I, lost in the sea
Beautiful waves splash on our face
You holding my mind
Lost in wonder
How would I figure you out?
The patterns of the universe
Everything is clear in my eyes

I'm spilling off –peeling off the paint
Drowned in the form, the seeker of the gates
Gates to higher freedom

Boundless Voices

Patterns of reality, close to the maker

Strange hum
Stranger within making him smile
Dipped in the wave
The colours wash his essence
Present moves slow

4. Coffee and blanks
Straight up younging, dreaming
On a cold night, singing – songs of the lost gods
I rewind the tapes to the old tales
The droplets smooth like jazz
The viscous starts, then hits hard
Plus the smoke, green if you know the feel

The year, 2018,
Stayed up screaming and dreaming
Young brother was lost in the dark
In his thoughts, all he could see was worlds
Some blank, some tasted sour,
In the lonely hours
Seated in a corner, plotting

So many reruns
The story, he didn't know the end
He saw something of a last breathe
The saddest take, he was the drop pale
Call it mystery or fate
The world works in different ways
Only the clearest minds can see the plays

He gained a touch, from the stars he felt
He could bend words right to left
With the slickest of rhymes
He set himself on a path
The first step took him to mars

Boundless Voices

Martian, Martian, he saw the lies
Of reality and duality of the human mind
Beyond his physical form, he transformed
Seeking the knowledge of the ancient world
The song placed on and on, the lost tapes

Half reality, half fantasy, divinity to his soul
Colour spill to the coffin, the great unknown
Just another story of resurrection
He found his soul

5.This is Art
Young, talented and black
Those were the words from mama
As she held my arm, she saw the future
Something I couldn't see
Now 22 years into the picture
Everything is clear from my eye
Grasp of the vision my birth prophesied

I'm scrambling for the masterpiece
My mama preached, put me on this path;
 it feels like redemption – second chances
Other times it feels like I'm jumping fences
Over the other side, the grass is greener
Fate is meaner

I can't complain, it kept me clear
From the suicide thoughts I dreamt
Life was horror, I saw red and terror
My heart was skipping beats
That was my hell, now it's clearer
It's something bigger, in the universe

With the infinity I converse
Trying to understand the picture
Every day is a new day
I understand little by little
With these words I say
It's a feeling beyond matter

Boundless Voices

Beyond the physical and what matter

It's something new
I hope to paint before my last breathe
 in a few moments and moments
Ring me the alarm
Wake up from my thoughts

A.A OLUWASEUN

He was born in Lagos, Nigeria. He is a prolific writer specialized in genres like poems, essays, novels and a lot of inspiring books

His creative wrings include," The lost love", "Perils of Christian Brothers" , "On my way to school", "The helpless", "Bride and Bribe ", and many others

1.We hope

Here lies the ruins of a once land of promise
An expanse that flowed with milk and honey
Now inundated by the blood of innocents
Sons and daughters of the same land
Much has gone wrong yet we wonder
If the darkest part of this night
Is truly the advent of dawn
We miss the sound of the morning bells
which toll the new dawn and hope
We miss times of safety
In what now, is the valley of the death?
The mere approach of twilight
Portends insecurity and danger
We miss joyous days, funny days
For all we know is sadness and silence
Through the regret, there is hope
Hope that our land would again
Flow with milk and honey;
The day we would wake the sound of the bells again;
Hope that we would be safe and secure;
Hope for a return of joy and gaiety
Tis our God – given and in alienable right
We hope, because we live amidst all these;
For where there is a will, there is life
He read, studied and mulled over his faith
He did his bidding, bowed his head in submission
But raising up his head, he saw an obscene picture

Boundless Voices

She was a breathing, temptation
He closed his eyes and prayed for strength.

2.The helpless
I see them as a family
But I got sidelined
I showed 'me love
They reciprocated with
clauses

...human with numerous
hearts
Clinched to evil darkness
Careless and fearless
Life is pain and equity

I'm not hopeless
Neither am I discouraged
I'll cry loud for help
My helpers are my haters

Revenge not on my path
I stick to my priority
Success! Success! Success!
One day is one day

MERCY MUTUNE

She was born on 6th April 2003 in Machakos, Kenya. She is currently chasing her dream at St. Martin Utithini Secondary School. She was introduced to poetry by Eric Kyalo who made her a great poetess.

1.Joy to the missionaries

Joy to the missionaries
You showed us kind gestures
You held our hands
You showed us steps of faith
Though a long journey
Today we celebrate
The fruits of our faith

Joy to the missionaries
We are so grateful
For your kindness
You spread Christianity
You hampered Islam
You abolished slave trade
Which was dehumanizing
And unfair
Causing misery and suffering to innocent Africans
Today we celebrate the fruits of our faith

Joy to the missionaries
You showed up great efforts throughout all situations
You failed in your mission
You were attacked by diseases
You faced language barriers
You faced rejection and oppression
But all in all
You never gave up.

Boundless Voices

2. Mum – Rosie

Mum
You're such an amazing creature
You carried me nine months
 in your womb
You bore all the pain
To the world you brought me
For six months you fed me
with milk from your furbished breasts

How affectionate are you?
You comforted me
Whenever I was so desperate
You sang sweet songs to me
You taught me how to count
You became my first teacher

You took me to church
And became my first mentor
You took me to school
And encouraged me to work hard
You gave me hope that
There is no gain without pain

What can I offer to you?
As a sign of my gratitude
What can I reward you?
To compensate your actions

Boundless Voices

I will always care and respect you
I'll always obey you
I'll love you my princes
To the moon and back
Because you deserve to be happy
I can't let you off my heart
Because you're my only mother.

3.My prayer

Hear my prayer O lord
Give ear to my supplications
In your faithfulness answer me
For I know that you're inferior
To the most eminent

Grant me serenity
To accept what unchangeable
And courage
To change all that I can
For you alone you're powerful
And merciful

Unlike the serpent who deceived Eve
By its craftiness
Protect me from all temptations
Grant me grace and strength
To bear all the troubles
In all situations I face

Oh, that you would bear
With me in a little folly
And indeed you do bear with me
In all difficulties I face in life
Hold me with your love and mercy

Boundless Voices

You have made me
 from nothing to something
From nobody to somebody
From nowhere to somewhere
I thank you my redeemer

4.My love – Joseph

Love does not encourage
Conventions and primarilies
Love is all about plurality
To the person you love most
And indeed you're the one
You gave me hopes
You promised me faithfulness
You're loving and caring
I admire to be with you
Bare footed on the grass
In the darkness dancing
'Bebup' music together
Holding each other tightly

You hug affectionately
You cherish my smiles
You make me feel like a queen
In our own house
I'd love you come and stay
With me
For you're my lovely darling
I'd never like to split up with you
Because I'm madly in love with you

You drive me crazy
You make me a compulsive leader
 Of romance

Boundless Voices

Because you're such a romantic
Babe
You create a whirl wind romance
Between us every time
You eradicate love hale relationship
Between us
How wonderful are you?
How romantic are you?
You 're my favourite valentine

5.My plight

To my fellow youth
I do say this to condemn
Although I had said it before
That you're in my heart
Together we are united
In building peace and unity
In our own nation
To enhance prosperity
Let's not be lured
By our greedy leaders
Who bribes us
By creating violence and instability
How shameless are they
May they they perish in darkness

Let's love our country
And be ready to die for it
And live in it
For the sake of it
Great is my boldness
Of speech towards you
Great is my boasting
On your behalf
For I'm filled with comfort
And exceeding jollity
In the all our tribulations
In the efforts we've made

Boundless Voices

To build peace and unity
To promote togetherness
To make one nation
That is politically stable

MARY DIANA

She is a simple idealistic provincial girl and a successful form four leaver. She is a poet and motivational speaker.

1.Dear self

Dear self
You have been through a lot
But endured it all
So fragile you were
Now a hand core you've become

Dear self
Don't seize being nice
For it won't cost you a cent
Just keep the spirit
Of spraying kindness to all

Dear self
Let not the past take the
 Better of you
 Cos you still have your
 Whole life ahead of you
And good memories to
 Create out of it

Dear self
Take nothing for granted
Always learn to
 Appreciate the little things
For you can never tell
What your future holds

Boundless Voices

Dear self
Struggle not to impress
The crowd
For what is yours
Will always find its way
To your heart.

2. IS IT A CRIME TO LOVE?

Some people love the sky
Regardless the weather
And so is my love for you
But you shattered me into pieces
While I was dying to collect you

If loving was a crime
Then I'll be behind bars by now
I gave my all to you
I thought I'll forever be your damsel
And you my fella

I had faith in our love
A picture I perfectly saw
Intoxicated by you I was
But you were not intoxicated by me
As I thought

I gave my all
But in return got a lifetime heartbreak
A scar that will take forever to heal
I didn't see this coming
For I was a bat blinding in love

I can't believe that
Am just a nobody, totally nobody
At my groom's wedding
Hearing you declare love to someone
Else
Breaks my heart even more.

Boundless Voices

3.THE YOUNG SHALL GROW

Listen my son
It's the end that matters,
Not the beginning
Life may not be easy
For it may tease us at times
Leaving us in despair

But remember one thing
The little shall be old
And good life you shall have
But for now son,
Just try to make lemonade
Out of this life is
 Giving you

You didn't choose to be
 An intelligent child
Neither did I want that
But since it can't be undone
You will have to cope up
With whatever comes your way

They say time
Is the healer for the wise
And everything has
 Its own time to manifest
So keep calm my son
For the future in you is bright.

Boundless Voices

4. HUNGRY PAIN

Rolling my sleeve I prinked my wrist
Ready to desert the room
But to no avail
For the pain inside me is overwhelming
And my thoughts are drowned back

Back to the days when
 You made it crystal clear
That it was over between us
Is the same day
Happiness seized
 Knocking at my doorstep

For the scars you left me with
Are still as fresh as daisy
In this abyss of pain
It's just me alongside this dreadful
 World
For the pain is what I have for breakfast,
 Lunch and supper

Day by day am dimming away
Since "It's over " thing had hit me
 Differently
Pain with no solution am facing
How I wish I could go back in times
When solutions used to present themselves.

FELIX MIHESO

He is a young scholar at Mount Kenya University. He is a writer of short stories, poetry, plays and play's director. His passion lies in all works of art.

1. AM KINDER LEAKING

Am kinder leaking
To be honest am done licking
I drip and trip but I get in the
 Trap just by bit, a beat kinder
Hip-hop beats trap
Am kinder broken, fragments of the
Fabric
Allure fragrance burning of the
 Far- brick
Stupid, yes, a prick leaking
 Heart a minor prick major D
Musical woven into a sharp major
Am torn in two I feel needling
I feel a need, always giving care
 Am stitch
"le s mots peasant tuer...."
That's French for ..... "words can kill"
Life happens.

2. REST IN PARADISE MAJOR

No matter how hard I try, all I do
Is cry
Doesn't matter if to myself I lie,
 Nothing is fine so why? Tears down
These cheeks and will be shedding 'em
 For weeks...

Sweet sixty, plus six known him for
 Less than sixteen
As father for four, a friend later a foe
A man of valour, fisting manners in
Me with iron
A generous general, showing love and
Hate in equal proportions
A father to many, a grandfather
To more
A light dimmed early
Now I ask myself, you insisted I
 Come and see you on your sickbed
You had a message for me
I blame myself I didn't come so am
Sad and depressed
So long Grand Paul....
Rest in paradise major.

3. STRIVE FOR LOVE

I begged for it
Seemed like I stretched my hand
Into her folded heart
I reached for it
Seems like I stared into eyes
That were looking to the inside
Of the owner's soul

Trauma is my solace
Love is my poison
Sorrow is my pillar
Happiness is my killer

I stretched my hand
She was snatched from my reach
This is my new norm
Yes
"Life happens...."

4. MY NEED
Nonchantly I grabbed my
Composure, gazed her in the eyes
And all I needed was a break up
Not because she ain't good for me
But the bridge was getting
 A little too high for me to manage
The fright
Just feel free, have your space
Instead of having an occupied
 Vacuum
She's no hussy nor a limbo buh my
Insecurities, overprotection and
 The likes won't fit in her world
She's just so different, so away
Yet close, so unbearable yet
Lovable and addictive
The acumen hurts, buh I'll
Recuperate with time.

5. DEAR MAMA

Ohh beloved me! Dear mama
Here fore see I come to you
Indeed of the suffering and pain
 I behold you child deep in pain
Nine months begotten
I believe I shall succeed
Even if I lack need
I got in mind at the moment
Whether joy or sorrowful moments
Your heavenly father is with us
And we shall live together as us

ANDRE KATCHEREKHWANYA

He is a Malawian poet, a critic and editor. He is also a computer specialist. He did business management at K $ M school of accountancy in Malawi.

1. STILL HOPING

Nothing to ease her crying

She is done waiting, searching

All she now is breathing

Love to her feels like teasing

She sours, seeing other

Lovers together walking

And wonders, when true love be

 Calling

For her to love again

And forget all of her rolling pain

She's seen loyal to every new love

Thinking that its' love from above

Putting everything into the relationship

But all she gets in return is

Unforgettable weep

But she still believes

That as long as she lives

Boundless Voices

From her kindliness, beauty and humbleness

Someone from the other end of

This earth,

Is gonna put a diamond ring on

Her finger

And only have her in mind to

Linger.

2. LUKEWARM CHRISTIAN'S SONG

Drawing to the edge of consumed dreams

Where up above the heavens seems eyeless

Down beyond the signs are ruthless

Uncomforted, with a crying so endless

All strides die to a sleep

The way seems long

No sweet song from the deep

To fill my hollowed soul

But fear that walks on hands and feet

The pain and the pain of my sins all meet

Being shut inside mocking eyes

Morning under the shade of hell's skies

Along my blood growing fire leaps

Hells fire is real leaving me only to gnaw

My teeth

Boundless Voices

The sin fed on my soul

Percolated it more

Loved it for so long

And killed it strong

3. ROTTEN BEUTY

She glistens in the starlight dreams

Her eyes glow young, staring blue

Perfectly chiseled and put in place

But all of these gather untimely death

To the dull minded fools

She soothes their sighing

With pendulous hips that hang a shaking

A rotten beauty in ready

And yet too many men dwell in her head

But all and in a dream walking dead

Little lips charmed with use of cosmetic bodies

But fade in seconds, with a thousand stolen

Kisses

In one's life, she 's the one to fill poisonous

Tears

But be careful, you with feelings in black and

White

Before she breathes dirty into your lungs

 For just a night

Boundless Voices

4. AFRICA/ AFRICANS

African heroes fought for Africa

Africa for Africans

Africa sweet real Africa

Africa not for non Africans

Africa sing one song of Africa

Sing it not with slaves owners of Africa

Africa liberate with Africa

Africa repatriate Africa

Africans end corruption chewing Africa

Africans end political impulse warming Africa

End xenophobia in Africa

Never sale Africa to non – Africans

Africa is for Africans

Africa colours still a peg of all misunderstandings

To non Africans who misinterpret Africans

Africa liberate with Africans

To teach non Africans who misinterpret Africans

The sweet morals of Africans

Boundless Voices

Stop breathing a pool of wars

That torment and kills innocent souls

Africa liberates with Africans

Your good fight must stitch all broken minds

Into one fined mind,

No more weeping, but kindliness in her

Healing we shall find.

By non Africans not from Africa

By Africans who understand Africans

5. WHEN WITH US

When with us, I see the rainbow in your eyes

And I feel like melting upon touching your

 Joyful tears

Tingling, mingling when tired we watch the stars

As they start to die

As they kiss the darkness goodbye

It feels like a game of clasping fingers

Before the sun

Our hearts leaping inside, from side to side

 With a run

Against the inside wind blowing all the

Sting of pain behind

It feels like breaking and forging our hearts

 A new

When with us, a coloured hue

We bloom each other's body with magical

Arms

Boundless Voices

Carefully in the midst of twinkling

Transference

JOSEPH FAITH IFEANYI

He was born in Abia state, Nigeria. He is currently a student at Nekede ND 2.

1.MY OATHS

My son

 Life is like a paper

Only your thoughts make you

 Live after death

The difference between failures

 And success is doing

Something or completely

Right

My greatest problem with

 Silence

It is that it can't measure

Wisdom and the cost of

 Foolishness

Education is the only person

 that don't lie after God

 Or judge wrongly or

Take bribe from you

Boundless Voices

2.HOUSE ON A HILL

House on a hill,

Forbidden kingdom

The course of house full of thorns

Sorrow and death

The three score

A hen and a weapon

Home of ignorance left by many

Home of spirits

Revenge, revenge, revenge

Only understood by one

A writer

Revenge the course house

Mystery to my village

My son don't live

But why father

My dream home

Boundless Voices

Only me and disabled man

Message from the grave

Revenge, revenge, revenge

I don't understand but I wrote

After writing and publishing

Peace was restored

Revenge, Revenge

Revenge, Revenge

3. MAN WITH TURFACE

Man with turface

Can't understand

Life was a mystery to man

Earth foods was education and eat

Mystery to black race

A courageous person

Wonder to the blacks

Ways are like two edges sword

My father's armor protects

 his son

Which began from nothing to something

Few words speak loudly

Library was more than school of thought

Eye of future

Avoid reader hobby

Boundless Voices

It was feeding from different information

 And communication

As tree can't stop fruits

So, his reading habit

4. THE FATHER'S BLESSINGS

Ointment of life

Seed of favour and foundation

Disciplined child

Lead to future unknown

Listen ear

Obedient Christian

Light to part way

Crown of life

Way to greatness

Key to adventure, creativity, road to possibility

Seed of grace.

Success in life, fulfillment of dreams

Bring progress and unity

Positive ideas, thoughts, resourceful materials, morals

My great part

Golden fruit all children desire

My father's abiya

Protect children

Boundless Voices

5. BLACK AFRICAN

Home of California and culture

Full of beautiful and amazing family

Origin of my kins

Full of sweet telent

And sound like minds

Honestly is the key they writer's weast bin

Full with great language and different

Episodes and trade, and tradition

One people, different culture and sound

Home of beautiful masquerade

Full with great language and customs

Home of idol

African pride

God of idol

Home of incations

Root in customs and culture

Boundless Voices

God loves

Home of hards, vegetables and roots

Full with straight vision.....

Full with different people

ERIC OMONDI

He was born in November 2000 in a family of five. He roots his humble beginnings from Siaya county.

1. LOVE MYSELF

I will stop loving
Until I love myself
I am tired of seeking validation
 From others
That I can't live without you?
How is it possible
I am the only one who can't live
Without myself
You made everything dark and gloomy
Even the cumulus are no longer
Cumulus but nimbus
Will not kill myself
But I will be patient with myself
I will not hurt my heart
But be honest with it
I deserve the best in life
Than pains and sufferings
I will not shed my precious tears
Anymore
But keep them for myself
I will stand for me
And build me
I will keep you in the past
And not my heart
I will be happy without you.

2. MY ANGEL

My angel, you are the beauty of my heart
Pray that you will be strong
Every negative arrowed words against you
Will not break your bones

I will protect you
With my life
Just as your mum tasted the bitter cup
Of demise to bring you to this world

Growing up
I will be your teacher
To answer all your questions
I will not shun from all your blows
I will take them by heart till my last breath

It is painful
I will not be able to protect forever
I hope you will learn to fight your battles
When I will be away.

3. MIRACLE

I remember
Everything calm and cordial
Just seated by the shore
You were embodiment of hope
I will hold you on my side

Now we are walking on our dreams
Pieces of every strategy that we ever said
It's before us as the beauty of the sun

We really fought a good fight
Everything was hazard at first
Our unity surpassed it all
We made our obstacles our slaves
Many had the same heart but couldn't make it
God of all flesh was on our side
Those sleepless nights before His presence
Rather than being engrossed in our own strength
Really worked miracles.

4. MY FACE

My face speaks a lot
These wrinkles and scales that covers it with
fidelity
Countless lines that only the deity can comprehend
The cumulus hear that silence in wisdom
Beyond what trend speaks of
Driven by edges and not changes

Speak of your current time!
Time had meaning
Its birth is present repulse our ancient
For there is nothing new under the sun
Complexity is embraced at every edge
But unity is vital throughout lifetime.

Your difference should bring you together
And not separate you
It all starts with love then understanding grows
 within.

5.STREET GIRL

I know everyone had once in their lifetime
Stepped on a thorn
But mine was different and dark
As a kid growing up in a street atmosphere it was hell

Couldn't hide the hyenas that stalk on me as
Their prey
Luckily enough to escape their peril
I grew as a child but inside
I lived a lioness
I had to fight my way through every hardship
Garbage was my livelihood
Dumped meals from the place was honey as
Time went
Inside me I felt as an angle less
A homeless street girl

I never looked down on myself
I knew success lies beneath my heart
I had to guard it with my breath
Not influenced by the surrounding but embracing
 The future
For there is illumination at the end of tunnel

Boundless Voices

------------------------THE END ------------------------

I am convinced that you have enjoyed reading this book.
For inspiring messages, motivational talks, leadership training, poetry for; status ceremonies, dedications and other events, kindly contact; **Destiny Ink Splinter**

Tel : +254741887616
email : Erickyalo517@gmail.com

www.noellorenz.com

Boundless Voices